Wanderings and reverie, memory and searching for a place to call home in the aftermath of Hurricane María, Susana Praver-Pérez turns to poetry. Through intertextuality and in conversation with the works of other poets and writers de aquí y de allá, these poems weave and stitch together moments of solace, joy, and healing.

—Vanessa Pérez-Rosario, professor at Queens College, editor, translator, and author of *Becoming Julia de Burgos: The Making of a Puerto Rican Icon*

We are daughters of diasporas. In *Return Against the Flow*, Susana Praver-Pérez invites us on a journey across seas, weaving her poems with other voices, rhythms, flavors, and images that seem to draw a map on her body with an ancestral force. With eyes wide open, she finds magic in life's daily experiences and faces the challenges of making a home in our colonized, Afro-Caribbean Borikén. Above all, this journey is an affirmation of the power of love beyond life.

—Dr. Mariluz Franco-Ortiz, professor at the University of Puerto Rico at Cayey, and member of Colectivo Ilé

Reading Susana Praver-Pérez's poems brings forth the sense that you're returning from a long journey, walking side by side with a friend. She fills your absences with color, sound, and imagery, like flavor on the page. Comfort and familiarity resonate in this book. She makes you feel at home in her words. She does not disappoint.

—Lady Lee Andrews, poet, artist, and proprietor of "The Poets' Passage" in Old San Juan, Puerto Rico

www.blacklawrence.com

Executive Editor: Diane Goettel
Book Design: Amy Freels
Front Cover Design: Susana Praver-Pérez
Full Cover Design: Zoe Norvell
Cover Art: "Taina: Spirit of the Coqui" by Tanya Torres

In June of 2023, Black Lawrence Press welcomed numerous existing and
forthcoming Nomadic Press titles to our catalogue. The book that you hold in
your hands is one of the forthcoming Nomadic Press titles that we acquired.

Published 2024 by Black Lawrence Press.
Printed in the United States.

RETURN
AGAINST
THE FLOW

POEMS BY

SUSANA PRAVER-PÉREZ

Para José.

Regresas

y regreso

con estas palabras

CONTENTS

INTRODUCTION

This is a story of departures and arrivals,
        comings, and goings.
This story is imprinted with stains
        of colonialism,
        disasters, and displacement.
This is a love story within a cauldron of crises,
        a battle waged with pots and *panderos*
        against austerity measures,
        against privatization of beaches,
        which belong to the people.
This is a story of rugs pulled out from under,
        of undermining a nation.
This is a terror tale of vulture capitalists,
        tax evaders, and neo-colonialists
        wearing leisure suits.
This is reportage of resistance, of return,
        of return as resistance, of return as love.
This is a love song sung to a *tierra santa*,
        a *mambo* splashed with *la mancha de plátano*.
This is the story of coquis singing lullabies,
        of knowing your neighbors—and their business,
        and they knowing yours.
This is a sacred tale of yearning
        transfused like blood in my veins,
        like a tattoo on my skin.
This is call and response, a response to a call
        I could no longer ignore.
This is a love song to Borikén…
        …*y a todas aquellas personas que la defienden.*

Susana Praver-Pérez
San Juan, Puerto Rico

& as we walk the beach you tell us of sea turtles

where the nests house
los niños soñando
in their eggs   waiting
for moons to lead their way
back to the ocean

where in the future
they will return
no matter where they have gone
remembering each grain
even if the beach is washed
                away

        & it all makes sense why I am here

        —*Isa Anastasia Rivas*
        (From "the poet leads me through Santurce,"
        dedicated to Susana Praver-Pérez)

BEAUTY

I was born with a birthmark
        shaped like Borinquen,
a brown island floating on the sea
        of my belly,
a curiosity under my fingertips.

My mother always called my birthmark
        a beauty mark,
turned it from stigma
        to stunning.

When I was ten,
a doctor convinced my parents
        this assemblage of melanin
        could endanger my future.

He cut the small map
        from my body,
stitched edges together,
        indurated, upended, and pink.

With time, the scar became smooth
        as sea glass,
soft and pliable, stretching wide
        as I grew.

By the time I turned twenty-two,
the scar embodied
       the shape of Borinquen,
suture marks suggesting
       surrounding islands:

Vieques, Culebra, Mona,
Palomino, Icacos, and more—
the entire Puerto Rican archipelago
       etched   again in my flesh.

RETURN AGAINST THE FLOW

In a small house made of cement
the cane cutter's children
became men and women
who departed, and when asked
"¿Por qué te vas?" avoided the eyes.

—Samuel Miranda (From "¿Por Qué Te Vas?")

An old man with hair dyed black
        like in better days,
                flashes a toothless smile.

He is so proud of his little house for sale,
shows me the cramped cocina and soot-filled sala
        all built with his very own hands.

The children he raised have all gone.
He sits on his porch alone
        watching Puerto Rico pivot
                on the point of a pin.

Where will you go? I ask.
¡Pa' fuera! he spouts, *Away!*

I have come to find a home
        of my own,
sink deep in this island
        that feeds my soul.

I am a car in the bus lane
driving against the flow
        on a one-way street.
People wave wild arms
        to stop me.

Nena, ¡¡Qué tu haces!? … What are you doing!?

They can't fathom why
I'd plant feet on cratered streets,
        entangle myself
        in an unraveling realm.

Their worries and warnings
        cleave my dreams,
        leave me questioning.

I see fresh green sprouting
        through cracked concrete.

        They show me old green mold
                invading houses.

I see red stripes and a single star shimmering
        in an aqua sky.

        They show me red blood
                of a nation crushed by promises.

Landscapes shift with every turn.

A hilltop mansion bathed in gold
          looks down on a sea of blue
                    FEMA tarps
          still topping fractured houses
                    long years
                    after the storm.

My mind is a cyclone of queries:

          How many chickens can run free
                    on urban streets
                    and still call it city?
          How many feral cats can fit
                    in a vacant house?
          How many abandoned pups can roam
                    beaches and backroads
                    before the call of the wild turns
                              all to dog eat dog?

          How can I tell if the sun piercing
                    the mangroves is sunrise
                    or sunset?

I pray for answers, I pray for Puerto Rico.

A wrinkled viejita in a well-ironed housedress
          rocks on her porch as I pass,
          wishes me *un buen día,*
          blesses me with her heartfelt *bendición*
                    while *Preciosa* plays softly
                              in the background.

BETTER HOMES & GARDENS: PUERTO RICO EDITION

Ramón had a way with women and words,
introduced me to Lucecita at the corner café.

Mi amiga, he named me, though we'd barely met.
Lucecita Benítez! Her name sparked

vinyl memories, eardrums, and soul.
Does she still sing? I whispered a bit too loud.

The diva's brow turned angry sea, turned
category three hurricane he quickly calmed.

We returned to our coffee, shared
stories from niñez 'til now.

He painted pictures in the air,
the grand home of his youth,

a splash of roses in the garden
his mother loved to tend.

We spoke of Spain—if he ever left,
that's the place he'd go.

Not stateside, with its Coca-Cola culture
and biased, blinkered eyes. *Pero, na'*—

He wasn't going anywhere—just counting
blessings, like stars mirrored on the sea.

We both loved houses, mourned
the ones ripped wide by brutal winds.

I laid bare my pockets,
shared my front-porch dreams.

Eye to eye, he vowed to find me
my garden of roses, my roof of flamboyán.

We wandered San Juan streets, the backstory of each
shattered house or empty lot like gossip across a fence:

> *Mira*, that full square block in front of SuperMax? Bought
> by an investor. Imagine the millions y *las palas* in their pockets.

> And that graffitied row on Calle del Parque? *¡Coño!* They offered
> *un montón,* but she won't sell to *vultures* flying circles in the sky.

We walked awhile in silence, shook our heads,
watched history unfurl like a lopsided prizefight.

My needs are simple, I said—*a bath, a bed,
a place to cook, close to my family and friends.*

*I'm not afraid to rescue
salt-stained walls, polish rusted rails.*

Como esa—I pointed to a rundown house
caked with cats, choked with vines.

Ramón had a way with women and words,
clacked the neighbor's door like a clave.

¡Buen día, señora! he sang, lauding her garden
and luck—the winds had spared her wooden house.

Her wizened face became that of a girl, opening
her barred door a little wider.

And the house next door? he asked. *Ay, mijo,* she sighed,
shaking her white-curled head. *Pues, tú sabes... La herencia...*

We sang the chorus in harmony, *¡Ay, yay, yay! La herencia...*
dead-end sinking us like a tsunami.

The laws of inheritance, penned to protect,
orphaned the house, legal title stuttering in the air.

Tú sabes, said the señora.
Tú sabes... y así, the stories begin.

A STORM NAMED MARÍA

Before the rain sliced like knives, she arrived
like a thoughtless guest—too early—
before the yuca was boiled and the table set.

She shouted her name from the street,
up through the second-floor windows,
voice like soot streaking drapes.

The virtues of her namesake, revered
in hallowed halls, disguised
her jagged nails and snake-filled hair.

She rumbled in,
slung her muddy boots
and bloat on sofas,

poured herself into bedrooms,
bent narratives, stained
scrapbooks with mold,

became backdrop
for family photos,
became a measure of time—

> Before and After
> Antes y Después

After the rain hacked like machetes,
she flew away, tin roofs tied
like wings to her scapulae.

She huffed her salty breath, left
her name etched on walls and trees,
like an explosion of graffiti.

     Now, when a lamppost tilts
     towards the sea,

          we whisper her name.

     When the washer overflows,
     bringing back those flooded days,

          we whisper her name.

     When traffic lights refuse to blink
     and cars jostle at street corners,

          we whisper her name.

     When the electric flickers and dies
     again, and again,   and again,

          we whisper her name.

Inscribed on 4,000 gravestones, "María"
is a mourner's rosary, a nightmare
from which we can't wake.

Yet, at daybreak, she sips café in our kitchens,
scratches at our skin to see what we're made of.
We don't know her by *doña* or *señora*—

          just her naked given name.

Nuestras casas ahora son
sitios arqueológicos
con las ventanas rotas
y fósiles digitales saliéndonos al paso.

****

Our houses are now
archeological sites
with broken windows
and digital fossils seizing ahead of us.

—*Nicole Cecilia Delgado*
(From "La Sed de los Oráculos")
Translated to English by
Roque Raquel Salas Rivera

CASTLES IN THE AIR

—May 2019

You could walk right by,
        not even see the lime-colored house
        amid thick emerald leaves.

Or its owner—señora of seventy years—
        her rocker in rhyme with a song of coquís.

Yellow-bloomed vines tangle grills on windows.
Mango tree shadows a battered tin roof—
        just a blue FEMA tarp
        between her and the rain.

Far worse, her sister's house next door—
        its roof torn wide by María's shrill wind.

Rain runs down walls mottled with mold.
Rust gnaws at a filigreed gate.

All her years as a lawyer are crumbling—
        she's perched like a bird,
        her front porch, her cage.

Pensions dissolve in fiscal default
        on an island held hostage
            by foreign dictates.

But this is her home,
        her haven,
        her castle,
jasmín y sofrito perfume the air.

New moon nights were splendid with stars
        before bright light
        high-rise buildings appeared.

Flamboyán y flores were felled to roll asphalt,
        parking lots spread to the edge of her green.

And now they want to bulldoze her house,
        demolish its walls and her dreams.

But each new day, aroma of coffee,
        the radio playing an old *le lo lai*,
she keeps the beat, the creak of her rocker
        repeating…repeating,
           a defiant reply.

CASTLES IN THE AIR (A POST-SCRIPT)

—April 2022

Doña Melisa is dead
and the Doubletree's done
what it all along said it would do:
bulldoze her house
and pave her land too.

Doña Melisa is gone
and the Hilton has bought
her old house for a song.
Her sister's house is next to go,
parking for cars lined up in a row.

Doña Carlota's laundry won't dry
sunshine blocked in a tower-filled sky.
The hotel wants to raze her house too,
but she turned on her heels
and shouted, *Fuck you!*

Predators fill the narrowing sky,
eerily waiting for neighbors to die.
They pick apart houses
and a barrio's life, talons
slashing like a jagged gold knife.

Doña Melisa was way down the list
of family homes that no longer exist.
Where once the streets of a neighborhood
flowed, now hotel boundaries
dead-end the road.

Though a block away as a blackbird flies,
they now need to spiral a maze
to arrive at the market
to buy some bacalao,
café, y leche, y un pan sobao.

As the cost to feed a family rises,
the soaring rent shocks and surprises
many who've lived on these blocks for years,
now floating away on a río of tears.

The secondhand store has turned
vintage boutique and local merchants
are squeezed out to seek new distant venues
to sell their wares, 'cause the landlords
see dollars filling the air.

From high in the sky
you can see the whole picture—
the claws, the beak, the deadening mixture
of money and power, post-hurricane sales,
a swarm of vultures gone off the rails.

where are the Puerto Ricans? / cuchifrito ghost town /
battery-operated citizenship / an island is not a tarmac /
a disaster is not a destination—

—*Denice Frohman* (From "Puertopia")

El negrito bonito
No encuentra trabajo
Está atolondra'o
Se siente muy bajo
Un tipo muy listo
Le dice al bonito
Que allá en Nueva Yol
Todo es mejol

—*Roy Brown*
(From "El Negrito Bonito")

yo veo a Brooklyn en las montañas of Juana Diaz
i see Ceiba Sur en la esquina de Union Ave and Hope St.

—*Isa Anastasia Rivas* (From "Yo Veo")

CUCHIFRITO AT MIDNIGHT

We were leaving Loisaida—
Not the town of Loiza Aldea
      on Puerto Rico's northern shore
      where cimarrones fled
          slavery's chains.
There was no surging sea
         before us,
      just an ocean of concrete
      still mirroring heat
         despite the midnight hour.

We were leaving Loisaida—
Not la calle Loíza
      that runs through Santurce,
      where scent of sofrito
         drifts on sea breezes.
That same smell was in the wind,
      but the air was thick
      with car exhaust
         despite the midnight hour.

We were leaving Loisaida—
New York's "Alphabet City"
where Avenue C is called *Avenida Loisaida*
      by Boricuas living
         in Puerto Rico's other "capital".

Avenue A could be for…*Albizu.*
Avenue B for…*Betances*
and Avenue C for…*¡Coño!*
      ¡Qué cara están las rentas!

So, Boricuas took that blighted neighborhood,
turned abandoned buildings back into homes
      for families to live and grow.

We were leaving Loisaida—
      to catch the train to Long Island (*la otra Isla*),
      the 1:00 a.m. from Penn.
We should make it—easy—
      blocks speed by walking in Manhattan
      on a warm summer night.

But then, we saw it—
      the blink of neon drew us in.
Patitas, orejas, chicarrón, rabos de cerdo
        all glistened
      in the *flash*ing*red*lights*.

¡Mira pa'lla!—¡Cuchifrito!—
      food from "home"
      steeped in larga tradición.
Scraps cast-off by los ricos
      made delicious by los pobres,
      made whole again.
Puerto Rican "soul food"
      in the middle of Nueva York,
      in the middle of the night,
        with a train to catch.

We were leaving Loisaida—
      the Loisaida in a city that never sleeps.
Where one can eat cuchifrito at midnight
      and make time and distance disappear.

We were leaving Loisaida—
     and the pleasure of finding
         the tastes of Borinquen
         in this city of steel,
    made the two-hour wait
        for the next train
            worth it.

CALDO CON KREPLACH

For those of us who sink our fingers into diasporic soil
chanting the names of lands we inherit through memory,
filling with seeds all that is missing, making a hybrid garden
of our new identities

—Peggy Robles-Alvarado
(From "For Who and Why")

Great-grandma Ana
was a stout woman
with peregrine eyes
that penetrate from a portrait
hanging in my kitchen.

Her bearded love sits
at her side, eyes gentle
as early morning sunlight,
a woven straw hat
in his calloused hands,
just before they crossed
the Atlantic.

I come from wanderers,
harvesters of almonds and figs,
tailors of torn seams
and mis-sewn borders.

I don't know
all the roots
of my kinked brown curls,
wonder

what tales foremothers
might tell
as I cook a pot
of caldo con kreplach.

We mingle, migrate,
cross continents and seas,
reflections in the water
like a sketch
on wet cement,
driftwood
and seagrass
as substrate.

We mix. We morph. We meld—
our scaffold a mesh
of diasporas,
our consonance and contrasts
each adding backbone
to keep us from breaking.

We are. We be. We become—
submerge in the fragrant soup
of existence,
nascent selfhoods
bubbling up
like dumplings,

fusion of flavors
bursting
with each exquisite bite.

I was adopted as an infant and didn't learn until age 18 that I was of Puerto Rican descent. It took me decades to believe that I had any right to that Puerto Rican heritage, but eventually, I came to feel that, even if I have a different relationship to my roots than other people do, they're still my roots! So, I moved to Puerto Rico to learn, to connect, to try to grow into a relationship with the generations whose blood is my blood.

That first night of my arrival in Puerto Rico, I chatted in self-conscious Spanish with the Uber driver who picked me up at the airport, and one word he said really hit me: "regreso." He was commenting on my "return" to a place I had never been, and the fact that he saw it that way made me feel like I belonged. People have been making me feel like I belong ever since.

~Anna Andresian (Volunteer at *Taller Comunidad La Goyco,* Adoptee born and raised in California, now living in San Juan)

CAMINANTE

Soft leather straps—
        a pair of sandals
found on winter's clearance rack,
"out-of-season" merchandise
        perfect for my plans.

Ready to roam,
I could nearly smell the loam
        of El Yunque,
feel the Caribbean kiss
my toes, sandals dangling
        from fingertips.

I was ready for embraces carefully
        stored like Christmas balls,
and the giggles of grandnieces
        trying to recall
        who I am.

But a virus paused my plans like a full stop—

I walked in circles alone, searching
        for blessings,
strolled my Oakland neighborhood,
lemon trees and bungalows
        my boundaries.

Today, sunlight floods my windows,
        news injects my view—

I'll soon dry my feet, damp with sea
       in Luquillo,
break bread with family,
cry at Titi Sara's grave.

I will wear out whatever life is left
       in these soles,
dare to dream again—
       fragile as that may be.

Irse y volver acaso te vuelve un extranjero.

Desconoces ahora tanto a Puerto Rico.
Caminando se empieza a descubrirlo.

****

Perhaps leaving and coming back makes you a foreigner.

There's so much you don't know about Puerto Rico now.
You begin discovering it by walking.

—Nicole Cecilia Delgado
(From "De Barrio Obrero a la Quince")
Translated to English by *Urayoán Noel*

THE HOUSE ON PÉREZ STREET

Every year, I wander these streets,
dabs of fresh paint
and stains of decay
equally edging the scene.

Restored Moorish arches stand tall
beside wood shacks
hacked to their knees
by the wind.

Abandoned buildings,
rusted gates, a vacant lot
that no one remembers who owns.

A yellow-plumed parakeet
pecks at weeds in sidewalk cracks.
Aproned neighbors debate what to do,
'til a doña in a housedress tucks the bird
between her ample breasts.

Flame-red flor de maga blooms
near blue garbage bins,
Friday-night cerveza cans overflowing
like a frozen river in the tropical heat.

Every year, I wander these streets,
looking for an open door, imagining
scent of my sautéed cebolla
wafting through windows,
mingling with Machuchal's aromas—
asopao and ocean air.

A three-legged cat limps
across the pavement.
Pink vines climb
the side of a house.
A settee in the marquesina
is upholstered
in my favorite shade of green.

An iron gate swings open.
A street sign gleams in the sun,
black letters on tattered white tin
plainly spelling my name.

LETTER WRITTEN ON A CLOUDY MORNING WITH A CUP OF YACONO IN MY HAND AND RAY BARRETTO PLAYING ON THE RADIO

My legs stretch wide
like a ballerina's jeté.
I have finally put in place
the bifurcated life
we imagined, *un sueño*
de pájaros preñaos.

My left foot lands among
California poppies, lavender,
and oxalis—named a weed,
though I find joy
in their yellow-petaled faces
and lemon-flavored stems.

Our rescued feral slinks
through tall grass,
her calico coat
still woven with wild.

Inside the Oakland bungalow
we bought when freshly wed
and the neighborhood was
flecked with crack houses,
there is steady light, a soft bed,
a fridge filled with yogurt,
tomatoes, and greens.

My right foot steps among
fallen fruit and leaves
of a mango tree, icon
of your youth,
then stomps roaches
that run for cover, scatter
in the Caribbean light.
There is ajo, cilantro,
y cebolla in the kitchen.

I finally leaped, *querido*,
into the vision we shared
but that I shredded
into cirrus clouds
from cumulous
billows overhead.

I am sorry, *querido*.
Your wild wings always frightened me.
But you weren't made
for a cold, northern cage.

I offer amends
with my own sort of wild—
a house bought sight unseen
in Borinquen, *amada tierra santa,*
where your ashes have surely settled
by now.

Fears fly off like seagulls.
Sea breeze slaps my face awake.
I pinch my arms and thighs.
My legs stretch and glide

across the globe glistening
like the polished wooden dance floor
in California where,
two seeds dreaming
in the wind, we first met.

CARTA DE AMOR

I was twenty-two and totally taken with the *títere* at the ticket booth.
Eyes full of flirt, José gazed through his cascade of curls, slipped me
into the sold-out New Year's Eve party—in trade for *just one dance*.

We whirled across the floor to sounds of El Sonero Mayor,
the skin on my back glistening beneath his hands.

My second-hand Spanish was no match for the Yoruba
and Taino-tinged version that clicked like a clave
from José's lips. He adored words, swore like a sailor.

On a crisp Oakland night, we exchanged vows—
branches of a sycamore our canopy,
the moon and stars, our witness.

In the month of the flowers 1979, we arrived in San Juan.
Workmen were pruning, painting, making the city shine
for the Pan-American Games.

Our first stop was the home of José's favorite aunt—
Titi Sara spoke on behalf of the family gathered
to meet *la chica* José had brought home.

I hear you are in love with my nephew, Sara said.
Sí, doña Sara, ¡Estoy enchulada! I replied.

Sudden smiles inspired me to further delight my in-laws
with words I'd learned listening to José:
¡Sí! ¡Estoy enchulada con cojones!

Grins twisted in shock. My stomach dropped.
¡Coño! ¡Carajo! I'd blown it!

Come evening, cuñadas y hermanos,
primos y sobrinos filled José's mother's home.
Reina de la cocina, doña María heaped
plates high with steaming rice.

Last served, my plate was a mound of crusty grains
scraped from the bottom of the pot.

I crumbled inside thinking
my vulgar tongue
had turned my suegra against me—
and punishment was a plate of scorched rice.

José laughed when I shared my fears,
explained the crisp *pegao* is a delicacy
fought for in his family—

To be served that by his mother
was an honor and embrace.

****

Our week was filled with treats—
We drank *guarapo,* sweet
        juice of crushed cane,
got giddy sipping *mavi*
        brewed from fermented tree bark.
I fell in love with *tostones*
        dipped in garlic sauce,
pasteles wrapped in plantain leaves,

mofongo bathed in *caldo*,
bacalao con viandas—
> *yuca, yautía, batata, malanga.*

And of course, plump *alcapurria*
> best enjoyed with an ice-cold beer
> under the stars in Piñones, the night air
> fragrant with cooking and ocean mist.

****

In Puerto Rico, the names of people delight
one's ear as much as the names of foods—

Three cousins, all sisters, all named María,
are called *Chary, Mili* and *Maggi*.
Artist friend Joaquin Reyes was *Chucho*.
Freckle-faced Marisol, *Maripecas*.

If your name doesn't morph
into *Tito* or *Fito* or *Lalito* or the like,
you may be called *Papito* or *Mamita*.

And, if you are lucky enough
to find your way into someone's heart,
you may be called *Negrito* or *Negrita*.

****

There is no doubt José made his way
into my heart, as I made my way into his.
There is no doubt he still lives in my heart.

When his soul left his body,
his spirit found other places to live...

    ...in the *tun-tún* of the conga,
      the playfulness of *bomba,*
      the way a *cha-cha*
      sways your hips.

      It lives in *el canto del coqui,*
      and the surf crashing
      on the sand in Aguadilla
      where he was born
      and where his ashes now swirl
      in the wind.

      And it lives when our son,
      born and raised in Oakland,
      proudly proclaims...he's *Boricua.*

When our son was little,
José would sing to him
'til he sang back—

      Dáme la mano paloma
      Para subir a tu nido

      Dáme la mano paloma
      (¡Qué chévere! ¡Qué chévere!)
      Para subir a tu nido

That's how you raise children
      with feet that can't stay still
      when the cadence of the drums fills the air.

That's how you keep love for the island alive,
      how you continue to live and thrive
      even when your body has returned to dust.

DELIQUESCENCE REFLECTED

Whose tears are these, Negrito?
Are they mine missing
      sweet scents of you?
Or are they yours,
      borrowing my body,
lamenting leaving yours
      too soon?

I know your constant smile
      in a faded photo
         isn't you.
I know eyes on me
      might see a woman
      whose mind has left
      this plane as I speak
         to your image,

but I am blessed
      to hear your voice
      in my ear,
blessed as you circle me
      in your spectral arms.

A MI QUERIDO NEGRITO EN SU DIA

December eleventh arrives
enrobed in fog and missing
and the warm cocoon of a cantaloupe room
you painted before
you became one with the wind, your ashes
dancing above Aguadilla.

Born in that place of little waters,
(though some say Aguadilla is not Spanish
but Taino for garden),
hijo de palmas, orquídeas, y olas del mar
crashing on ivory sand. Your song
ran along stone rivers,
Rio Piedras where you grew,
sweet mangos bursting as they rained
upon your flat cement roof.

I place a slice of that fruit
like a heart
upon your altar
and a flag of your beloved
Borinquen unfurled
black and white in a sky
like leche de coco that once fed
your vibrant flesh.

En el cielo
encancaranublado,
your soul, still bright,
veins the gift of you
like rivulets of molten gold.

PA'QUE TÚ LO SEPAS

No nací en un hogar puertorriqueño
    pero crecí como mujer en uno.
El boricua quien me robó mi corazón
    sembró sus raíces en la tierna tierra de mi alma
El flamboyán que creció
    es precioso.

SO THAT YOU KNOW

I wasn't born in a Puerto Rican household
    but I grew into a woman in one.
The Boricua who stole my heart
    planted his roots in the tender soil of my soul.
The flamboyán that grew
    is precious.

SANCOCHO

My son has a name a full hand of fingers long.
When the DMV made him fan all his names
        on a table, like a gin-rummy flush,
      he asked,
What were you and Pa thinking!?

What we were thinking was
        to paint the map of your being
            in such bright letters
        you would never lose yourself,
            never lose us,
        nor your grandparents, tus abuelos,
        your great-grandparents, tus bisabuelos,
            as you walk in a world
        where accent marks are seen as rubble
            to stumble on,
        and the roll of an "r" an aberration.

We stamped you with the world of my ancestors,
        or what we knew of it—
        after a genocidal war
        destroyed the shtetls of Europe
        and yanked those roots from the soil.

We gave you my paternal name
        which may not really be
        my father's name
        or my father's father's name,
            but a name

a clerk at Ellis Island approximated,
a name that in Russian may have been
Pravda—meaning *Truth*.

The truth is hidden in an uprooted name.
We hold on tight to our names, always
seeking the truth.

Y tu Papá stamped his name and his roots
on you, and on me too, embossed
an ever-present *Pérez*
on birth certificates,
marriage licenses,
and as you well know, mijo,
drivers' licenses.

Pérez is like *Smith* in the Spanish-speaking world,
but instead of the beautiful
cascade of syllables it is,
PÉ-rez is puréed into *per-EZ*
by English-speaking mouths.

Never let them tell you how to say your own name—

It is yours.

It is yours, and Papi's, and now mine.
It belonged to abuelo Mateo who lived
in a wooden house with no hot water in Moca.
Y tu bisabuelo who walked those fertile hills barefoot,
cracked soles caked with red soil.
Y tus tatara abuelos whose names were scrawled
on the front page of a Bible with a pencil
sharpened with a machete.

Your roots reach deep and far
        in a land whose sweetness
                was sucked by cane fields
                        and colonizers.
Roots that spread
        like woody lianas
                and flowering vines
                        in El Yunque.
Roots that flow
        through the halls of our home,
        shape glistening sulci in our brains,
        thickly seasoned braid of blood
                beating like a bomba drum,
                        strumming like a balalaika,
                        dancing like verbs
                              in our veins.

TATTOO IN TWO VOICES

My son just told me
he's got a tattoo…

I'd been waiting for the other shoe
to drop for a decade since
a 2 a.m.   long-distance
call—

Mom, where was Papi's "J"?

¿¿ *Por qué* ?? Are you planning to get a tattoo!!??

Nah. Just askin', been meaning to ask for years.

His left calf, mijo…he liked things
with his initials: a golden "J" pendant,
un cuaderno de cuero,
white cotton pañuelos…

Where exactly?

On the widest part of his batata—he did it
at about your age—a teen
with ink and pin,
hid it
with stray pen marks
on his skin.
Imagine the drama
when Abuela found out!

How big? Capital or nah? Blue or faded black?

Blue. Mayúscula. A thumbnail tall.

A'ight…

You got me thinking
about your Papi, mijo,
how he loved
to make things:
bookshelves and tables,
sandbox and beds.
Do you remember
the playhouse he built you
by the camellia?

I forgot… 'til just now, thought
I just liked climbing the tree.

And how he liked to clown around!
Do you remember
balancing on his shoulders
while he rode a bike
up and down Titi Guille's street
in Aguadilla?
You were maybe five…

Do you remember?

Ma, you're always asking if I remember…

My son just told me
he's got a tattoo
done with blue ink & a pin   a "J"
on his left batata
his very own *mancha
de plátano.*

MAY IT BE

This gift of waking
is the same—
but gathering twigs
and cooking by flame
impacts the earth more softly
than our modern morning rites.

Symphonic swell of birdsong
paints a crisper air
than highway hum.

Dear atom, dear molecule, remind me
we are still made of stardust
as fire ash fills our lungs
and green-scented mornings
are sacrificed
to avarice and ease.

How, sweet son, do I share
the secrets of centuries
when monarch migrations
teeter on extinction
in our lifetime?

How do I light candles, praise
forward-flowing ties,
generation to generation,
as if guaranteed?

I thrill to see the timeless
glow of love
in your young eyes, delight
as you taste the sweetness
of heirloom figs,
see wonders strung like rosaries.

I want to become an ocean, buoy the future,
seaweed swirling like a bomba skirt
around my waist, plankton
glistening on my skin.

I pray to quell rising seas that swallow islands.
I pray that grass sprouts on scorched hills.
I pray for the monarch, rhino, sea turtle, lemur.
I pray for the earth's healing
so that you, querido hijo, may know
the vastness of the sky's blue and the fullness
of the river's length.

NO SMALL LOVE

(After Sonia Sánchez)

this is no small island
you see   this 33 by 100-mile splash of green
            this island is large, long, a syncopated song
                        a sizzling, crimson flamboyán

this is no emerald speck
you see   floating between two swirling seas
                        Africa & Spain
                        twirled
                        Taino DNA
                        &
                        new perfection
                        grew

this is not a flash   of light
                    drifting
            in a jet-black   night

this is loam & cordillera
caña, plantain, cascade   of
                        calloused hands

this is no small love
you see   this land   of
                    Maelo
                    El Topo
                        &
                    Don Rafael

passion-flavored verse
                plumeria-scented breeze

this love is a porous arc   of palm trees
                pours itself   on balmy skin
                like waterfalls on obsidian
this love figure-eights   its hips
                unlocks   rusted gates
                drips guarapo from its lips
this love   is where I am
                hermana
                negrita
                mami
                mi amor   you see

this is no small love

You clap when you arrive here and cry when you leave. It's the so-called Isla del Encanto. Living here, this land feels more like a breathing entity to me. It revealed itself as a teacher, mother and goddess, and I observed, listened and learned. I refer to my process as a "rematriation" versus repatriation because I recognize how this land serves as my teacher to decolonize me and restore me back to my essence. Rematriation more accurately refers to this journey as it is a literal return to the womb.

—*Yasmin Hernandez* (visual artist)
From her blog: rematriatingboriken.com

my heart lies onethousandsixhundredtwentyfive miles
    on the shores
my parents made love on

I will find it there
when I return

—*Mario José Pagán Morales*
  (From "*onethousandsixhundredtwentyfive*")

AT LAST

Quiero reintentar
acuchillar mis miedos
dejarlos desangrar…

—iLe (From "Caníbal")

For decades, I have longed
for this island
that grew within me
from a tiny seed—yet
feared fusing
with a land
so ravished
and raw.

I have wet my toes
and walked away
so many times, afraid
of algae blooms
and riptides.

But desire cycles
like a moonrise
that paints sparkles on the sea,
singing like a siren
in the dark.

Pulse like a tinglar heart,
I breathe deep—dive
wild waters,
swim against currents,
yield at last,
to your call.

LEARNING A HOUSE

I arrived late at night, no electric
for light, lullaby a choir of coquis.

Come morning, coo of doves
and rooster's crow woke me
as the sun's first beams
lit Santurce's narrow streets.

I unsheathed each window
like a child tearing open gifts:

> Bottle-green leaves of an almond tree.
> Yellow flowers whose name I'm yet to know.
> A clucking hen and her chicks foraging bugs.
> Bees buzzing in blooming vines spiraling
> > over a fence.
> Feral cats, rail thin and crooked boned, lounging
> > on the roof next door.

In the living room, reek of cat pee rises
from a leftover sofa. Entry, a broken window—
trail of claws streaking gray walls.

Quickly I learn
the local biota:

> the giant cucarachas,
> the lightning-fast lizards that eat the cucarachas,
> the gliding birds that eat the lizards,
> the homeless cats that eat the birds,

the murmur among neighbors
about someone killing the cats,
the murmur among neighbors
about doña Irma who's gone
to a "home" and the long-neglected house
where I've landed
to fix and clean,
haul and weed,
salvage
a decades long dream.

WHO, WHAT, WHERE, WHEN, WHY, AND HOW OF A HOUSE

No one told me
>> whose clothes hung in the closet,
>> with a glass bowl of pennies
>> and a set of gold teeth.

No one hinted
>> what happened
>> to the dirty front windows,
>> smashed and scalloped like leaves.

Nobody knows
>> where the water main's buried,
>> or the names of the walls'
>> painted hues.

No one recalls
>> when the house was last lived in,
>> or when rain last leaked
>> through the roof.

No one said why
>> locks were picked, pried, or broken—
>> just a padlock and chain
>> now doing their best.

No one spoke
>> of muffled wisps of fantasmas—
>> but I've dealt with spirits
>> and knew how to lull them to rest.

LA LIMPIEZA: INSTRUCTIONS
FOR CLEANSING A HOME

Begin with a broom and sweep out
the corners—flaked rust from old rejas
and traffic's black soot.

Continue with mop and pink
Fabulosa—blossoming
fragrance filling the rooms.

On hands and knees, scrub stray
marks and manchas, stiff bristles
biting   terrazzo floors.

Still, there are stains—orange rust
in the shower—seek super power—
spray *SacaTó*.

Febreze the mattress, bleach out
the curtains, ditch cardboard
boxes   where roaches breed.

Empty the closets, scrub out the toilet,
replace the light bulbs,
patch up the screens.

Degrease the kitchen, *Dawn*
for the dishes, *Windex* the windows,
wipe down the stove.

Agua de Florida,
sage at the doorway,
flame a white candle—

Bendiga this home.

FULLY EQUIPPED KITCHEN
(MAGNET POETRY ON THE FRIDGE)

[listen] to   the   [music] [under] your [skin]

    [praise] the [blue] [song]   of the [morning]

    [learn]   [secrets]   of [delicious] [love]

      [question] the [urge]   to   [hide]

[howl] your [humid]   [poems]

   [insist]   your [brilliant] [voice]

       [into]   the [world]

SABORES

el agua sabe   un poca a tierra
la leche sabe   a teta de vaca
el pollo   a plumas
las chinas   al árbol
la lechuga del país
                          al sudor
                          de las cejas

el casabe sabe a manos Taínas
el coco   a África
el flan   a España

la lluvia sabe
          al cielo azul
el aire   lleva adobo
          de vida

FLAVORS

the water   tastes a little like soil
the milk   the flavor of udder of cow
the chicken   of feathers
the orange   of tree bark
local lettuce   like sweat
                        from a brow

casabe tastes like hands of Tainos
coco   like Africa
flan   like Spain

the rain tastes
          like deep blue sky
the air   is flavored with spices
          of life

TERRITORY

The little brown chickens have fled
the empty lot next door, pushed out
by buff white roosters and hens,
the muted croon of gallitos replaced
by giant gallos' crow.

If the beloved cock wasn't
an icon of Borinquen,
this scene outside my window
could be a metaphor
for displacement
on the island.

Maybe imported iguanas
that overrun the land
and wreak havoc on the harvest
are a better metaphor.

The other day, I saw an iguana
squashed flat on a hot tar highway.
Maybe that's a metaphor too.

THROUGH THE CRACKS

En la esquina de Diez de Andino,
      a barrier
keeps pedestrians off the sidewalk.

We walk in the street
      for safety,
balconies above
      shedding layers
            like a molting snake,
      rusted rebar akimbo
         in the air.

El agua y los años crumble concrete,
      brittle as fraying lace.

I see the sky through a broken techo,
      alcanzo el cielo con mis ojos.

Graffiti cascades on this corner—

    una rana con gafas

Rafi ama Marta

¡ FUERA LUMA !

BASTA YA

City workers sprayed it all
        a near-white gray,
        whitewashing decay
like 1980s faux flower decals
        on boarded windows
                of burnt-out buildings
        along the Cross Bronx Expressway.

Memory is a highway on a bridge to the past.

Through a broken roof, I see the sun—
        the same sun ancestors greeted
                from their balconies,
        saludos and scent of café
                wafting from below.

The morning's *buen día* is a threatened species
        falling through the cracks.

I want to sink into the cushions of a rattan sofa
        in the long gone sala de mi suegra,
        family thick as a bush in full bloom.

Nostalgia is a blessing and a curse—
        a buoy and an anchor
        wrapped around my limbs.

What should I clasp
        in my anxious grip?
What weight to let sift
        like sand through my fingers?

Even as a broken techo trickles rain
            down a stained wall,
we see the sky—the stars
            spreading across the night,
                    remember
            we are touchpoints
                    in the ether.

EAR HUSTLE

Rafaela speaks
to her dog, the clip of her
words float
through my window:

SIEN-ta- te, SIEN-ta- te

I hear the lilt,
diagram the line,
discover
a pair of *dactyls*.

My neighbor speaks
to her dog and her voice
becomes drumbeats—
two metrical feet dancing.

SOME HOMES HAVE WATCHDOGS,
MINE HAS BEES

Entering my threshold,
a friend's eyes flashed fear—
bees buzzed in blossoms
vining my gate.

Cavalcade of floral sprays,
graceful tendrils lifting
like pinkies at High Tea,
a calm sea of pink and green.

The flowers bend themselves
into bouquet, birthday crown,
blanket of splendor
hiding razor wire.

The vines mislead
like a street-corner swindler,
'til you hear them called
daña finca, damager of lands.

You won't find *daña finca*
in the dictionary—though
people spew those words
when the vine kills their trees.

Bees alight on blossoms, lick
pollen from a thousand pink cheeks,
make their sweet brew
while we fear their sting.

To dread bees and embrace
beguiling vines
that strangle crops and trees,
trades Heaven for Hades.

MADRE TIERRA

I am soft   soil
        and hard   rock.

My tectonic edges

      curve,
           cradle,
                journey.

I move,   slow
dance, drift, hum   something
        so sacred

      it can't be written down
        only passed down

      in a whisper.

Look for me

      beneath
        all this concrete
          and glitter.

Find me

      among
        the ceiba
          and yagrumo.

NAVEGANDO

(For Gisela Rodríguez)

Yesterday didn't feel like Navidad as I traveled
through the stratosphere, seven miles in the air,
        navigating two worlds.

Christmas dawn, a hammer pounding concrete
startled me from sleep, un aguacero let loose
        turning blue Borikén skies to gray.

Rainfall ramped the coquis' call,
cicadas added their trill, and the day danced
        to Atabey's song.

Island climate is a carousel—
el cielo escampó, the sky sang turquoise
        while the sun hummed harmony.

****

Boxing Day, I wake to Oakland's quiet chill,
a lone robin chirping, muted by glass,
        raindrops swirling on the window.

Here in California, Salad Bowl of the World,
I joyously fill my fridge with greens—
        lettuce can be a luxury in San Juan.

****

Island-grown produce takes tortuous treks to the table.
Santa Isabel's tomatoes breathe Caribbean air until picked
        and sent across the sea to the States.

There, the red orbs are packed in crates and shipped
back to Puerto Rico at sky-high prices
        for shoppers with thin billfolds to buy.

This is colonialism in a shopping cart—
ricocheted tomatoes, Kellogg's corn flakes,
        pink-cheeked Santas, fake-snow-flecked pines.

This is domination spooned like sugar in our coffee
and the candies alcaldes throw from their cars
        to kids on the corner for Navidad.

Outside the supermarket, a white-haired woman
bangs a ladle on a soup pot, shouts *¡Basta ya! ¡Basta ya!*
        And the coquis loudly sing the chorus.

ODE TO TITÍ

Tití Sara could squeeze juice from a dime.
And when she ran out of dimes,
Tití could suck sap from a centavo.

They say oil and water don't mix,
        but Tití knew how
to water aceite vegetal, make it last
'til her next paycheck.

Tití opened her triple-locked door,
embraced me
in her freckled arms—
        Aquí tienes tu casa.
        Siempre.

As soon as I settled,
I skipped to the market—
        café y queso,
        piña y parcha,
slipped fine Spanish olive oil
        into my cart,
succulent frill
        for her cupboard.

¿¡Por qué compraste tanto!? She queried
        as I hauled in the shopping,
        voice the tone of her short copper hair.

You gonna eat all that? She asked.
We gonna eat all that! I replied,
      storing the rice with a wink
          of my eye.

Tití cooked arroz con gandules,
      plátanos fritos,
      pechuga de pollo
      steeped in sofrito.

No sooner than plates were laid on the table,
we heard a *tok-tok tok!* at the door.

¡Buen día Sarita!

Olga, from down the hall,
in house dress and shawl, to borrow
      some olive oil,
¡Si me haces el favor!

¡Cierto! said Sara, jumped like an athlete,
      poured half her flask of oil in a jar.
¡Toma! she said, with the grace of a dancer.

      Así fue Tití.

If Tití had two dollars, she'd give one
to a tecato trembling on the corner,
spend days and nights aiding the ill.

But where was the aid when Tití got ill? After María
      knocked out electric, left her
      sin agua, eating canned tuna
      'til her intestines jammed.

Where was the aid? Stuck in her building,
        car soaked to chassis in hurricane surge.

Pallets of water left on a runway,
        while Tití and thousands withered
          with thirst.

Tití died
        en el Hospital del Maestro
        surgery soiled by darkness and heat.

Dancing barefoot with angels, al campo santo,

      Así fue Tití.

The shoes she left, too huge to fill,
        stand empty
            frente al Capitolio
            and the White House lawn,
                silent witness
            to what went so wrong.

To the bad times,
give a happy face,
place a red amapola
in your black dark hair.
Revive the mummies,
the dead,
burst the bodies
out of the coffins
let's all walk to the plaza
this final time
paint with silver starlight
the ancient songs...

—*Victor Hernández Cruz*
(From "Puerto Rico")

STILL(WITH)LIFE—WOMAN WITH
ROOSTER

(An ekphrastic poem inspired by
a mural by Luis Pérez)

Eyelids droop—
not like junkies
slumped and scratching
scabbed and sun-burnt skin,
but with sober silence
soaking the air after storm
turned all to ruin.

Body bare—
not like sunbathers
on Condado's beach,
curated bodies
coated with Bain de Soleil,
but nakedness of wind and want
and bitter sweat of dread.

Rooster in arms—
not a blue-plumed cock
wearing spurs, sporting men
betting next month's rent
on a better chance,
but a rooster that dreams
a hen with golden eggs.

On a tall concrete wall—
not a factory facade
in Tras Talleres, barrio peppered
with printers' and mechanics' shops,
but a wall turned auburn phoenix
on Santurce's rebirthed streets,
acrylics flowing like amniotic fluid
                in the muralist's hands.

LETTER TO "LA CASA DE FLORES ROSADAS"

I gaze at your photo
pinned as screen saver
on my phone,
your front windows
like eyes staring
from under canopies
that flutter like lids
in the breeze.

You watch for my return
to Borinquen.

Your front gate is locked
like a stoic jaw, a mystery
to passersby—but I know
your magic—the way
a carousel of arthropods
circle your rooms
according to who's there:

Giant spiders scampered
across white walls—
their long dark legs shadowed
steps of a jarring guest.
When he left, the spiders left too.

Mosquitos that rarely bite me
throng with hungry mouths
when my sweet son arrives.

And then, flying termites—
spiraling through the living room
as if a flock of birds
in a painting on the wall
had suddenly sprung to life.

I swatted at the flapping things,
crashed my hand as I crushed
wings against concrete.

My fingers still hurt
with every bend—every throb
pulsing thoughts of you.

Now that you sit alone,
Do any creatures swarm?
Do the roaches dare
flurry through the kitchen
or nest in the closet
with the extra shampoo?

Does Atlantic wind filter
through louvered windows,
make dresses in my closet dance?

Does el señor who sells produce
from his farm still park
his pickup by your gate?

I cooked with his bounty:
berenjena, batata, yuca, calabaza.

When I left, I turned off all the breakers,
except the one for the fridge, freezer
saving sancocho to serve in celebration
the day you welcome me   home.

UNGENDERED MUSCLES

This is what remains,
eyes that have watched
how departure returns

—Samuel Miranda ("Departure 1")

Las señoras see me
sling my suitcase
      into the overhead bin,
watch it slide
      back onto my shoulders
         like a retreating tide.

Espérate, they counsel,
Espera por un hombre—Wait for a man—
    schooling me
        in the tools of survival
        when muscle is coin
           of the realm.
I lower my suitcase,
Machiavellian winks
behind abuelita glasses
      guiding my moves.

I stand in the aisle waiting,
assessing biceps and brawn,
coyly croon: *si me haces el favor*...
      and my suitcase glides
        into place.

The council of elders watch
          with crossed arms,
nod their approval, and I settle
          into my gray leather seat.

Half a day of blue sky later,
we land on the tarmac
y las señoras initiate
          the requisite ritual
          for arriving in Puerto Rico,
jubilant applause
          shifting a certain something
                    within.

Changing airplane air
          for scent of ceiba and sea,
my glasses fog
          in the steamy heat.

Arriving home, the coquis sing
          their greeting.
I haul my bags to the second floor,
          no *hombres* around
          to *pedirles un favor.*

Months of rain have littered the curb
          with debris. Water pools
          like a moat by my door.

Shovel in my calloused hands,
          I dig and scoop,
toss loam and leaves to the side,
          make way for water's flow.

The scrape of my shovel
          reverberates
off canyon-like walls
of our closely spaced houses.

The clatter brings a neighbor to her gate.
My hair untamed, mud streaking my cheeks,
I look up to see doña Nivia's quiet face
          now lit with a smile, eyes dancing.

¡Ja! ¡Mira pa'allá! ¡Una mujer macha!
calling me "man-woman"
          as if the council of elders
          were seated on the sidelines
and me, the new neighbor,
          squirming on the witness stand.

I am still waiting for the verdict:
          whether I have broken
                    unspoken rules
          or cracked open a door
                    to new ones.

SANA, SANA, COLITA DE RANA

Doña Rafaela sings
acapella to coquis—
grows bromelias, little frog nests,
'neath her cocotero trees.

Doña Rafaela knows
mañana must be colored green—
When hurricanes whip eruptive winds,
she shelters precious plants and seeds.

Doña Rafaela feels
the heart of every stone she sees—
a steward of Borinquen,
a healer, like the honeybees.

PROPIEDAD HORIZONTAL

Te digo, there will be days
when you won't have water,
Natalie divined when I first moved in
   on the second floor.

Layered like stratified stone,
our flats are two mirrored halves
of an aged concrete structure.

Downstairs, Sancha barks, guards
Natalie & Nivi's home. The sisters
   have lived here a dozen years, yet
this is the first time
   los altos y bajos
   are working as one.

Three graying women—together,
our years gather more than two centuries.
Our brawn, now waning, has hauled
   our own *altos y bajos*
   across continents. And here
   we are, nesting
   on a narrow street in San Juan.

Smile blooming on her face,
Natalie convenes the first meeting of
   mujeres poderosas
     por ayuda
      mutua.

We revisit the problem of water—
        the sad story of Irma,
bucket in hand, *pidiendo, ¡Bendito!,*
        un poco de agua.
When pipes pulse weakly,
water can't reach the second floor.

¡Y la luz! Electricity retreating & raging—
        appliances sparking,
        groceries rotting,
                while LUMA *no hace na'.*

The infrastructure is a mesh
        of potholes, sagging lamp posts,
        threads of broken safety nets
           flapping in the air.

Te digo, Natalie says, *nadie nos va a cuidar,*
        we, *nosotras mismas,*
        are all that we have.

We are three graying women
        living in a gray house
           from the last millennium.
But we look toward the future,
        reach to the sky
           where nature dangles
              answers
        on an island bathed
           in sun, water, and wind.

There is no lack of water here, but rain
is lost to damaged dams.
Desalination, de rigueur on neighboring islands,
supplies just smidgeons of sweet water here.
Sun and wind power's toeholds,
tentative and frail.

Self-reliance threatens
the status quo—colonialism
cultivates dependency
to survive.

We are *mujeres poderosas,* more capable
together,
more powerful
knowing

self-sufficiency
and sovereignty
are sisters.

AUTORIDAD DE ACUEDUCTOS Y ALCANTARILLADOS

Buen día.
Usted se ha comunicado con
la Autoridad de Acueductos y Alcantarillados.
For English, press 1.

1

Gracias por llamar
a la Autoridad de Acueductos y Alcantarillados...

EL PLOMERO ES EL PRIMO
DE UN AMIGO BOMBERO
QUIEN TOCA EL PRIMO

**(The Plumber is the Cousin
of a Friend Who Plays the "Primo"
—the Lead Drum in Bomba)**

Praise the cistern—I have water.
Praise the pump that cedes water
to the second floor. Praise the plumber
who swept the pipes and let the pump
yield water. Pump in Spanish is *bomba*—

En Borinquen, bomba es baile.
En Borinquen, bomba es vida.

Praise the *bomberos* who beat skins
stretched tight over barrels. Praise
the drums that chant ancestors' rhythms.
Praise the *primo* that sings dancers' stories.
Praise the stories that carry *cultura*—

En Borinquen, bomba es cultura.
En Borinquen, cultura es vida.

DANCING BOMBA EN LA GOYCO

For those of you
who still wonder why we dance,
I have to tell you—
joy is a quinto in the dark.

—Rich Villar
(From "Manifesto After the Storm")

I strain to hear el maestro's words,
  inflections careening
  off concrete walls,
  a flash aguacero rumbling.

He weaves yoruba y español,
  centuries of Puerto Rican history
  wedged like shims
  in the slim caesura between words.

  maraca, barril, y cuá
  sicá, cuembe, yubá

He shares a dancer's terms—
  pasos, piquetes, el repique,
  an arc of energy
  as large as one's wingspan
  even with fists
  planted on hips,
  aún así.

I listen with poet's ears, learn
  to mark one's space

with the tips of *los dedos corazón*—
>> the heart fingers, so named
>> by the Greeks who believed
>> a vein ran from the longest digit
>> to the center of one's heart.

I stretch my arms wide,
>> fingers reaching
>> beyond the walls.

I inhabit my body, feet
>> in the beat of *sicá,*
while my mind travels
>> through time.

I remember children's voices
>> bounding off these walls
back when this centro cultural
>> was a school
>> y mi suegra lived
>> on the second floor
>> of the building next door.

We told time by the glee of recess banter
>> in the playground below her balcón.

Floating in amber,
>> the past dances
before me, invisible
>> a los demás.

Bittersweet reveries
drip down my arms,
>> pool at my feet—

one, two, three *y ¡Tá!*
Golpe caja on the drum—

Tún, ta-ca-ta, Tún, taca-ta, ¡Tá!

Language of the drum,
lingo of the body,
idiom of *mi dedo corazón*
       pointing
towards the treetops,
       reaching
for recuerdos
       nesting
in the leaves
of my heart.

¿CÓMO QUE LA FIESTA DE LA CALLE SAN SEBASTIÁN ESTÁ CANCELADA?

My mother rode elephants in the circus.
When I heard music and saw dancers on stilts
coming down the street, I ran out of my house
into the drizzle and joined the parade.
Circus flows in my veins.

—Susana Praver-Pérez (January 15, 2022)

Plena, plena, plena, va
SanSe en Machuchal

Panderos down the narrow streets
Dancers tall on stilted feet

Plena, plena, plena, va
SanSe en Machuchal

Cabezudos in the crowd
Raindrops fall from thick gray clouds

Plena, plena, plena, va
SanSe en Machuchal

Can't let traditions fade away,
Fiesta en la calle, ¡¡eh!!

Plena, plena, plena, va
SanSe en Machuchal

Tito Matos in the lead
SanSe en Machuchal

In 3 days' time our hearts would bleed
SanSe en Machuchal

Plena, plena, plena, va
SanSe en Machuchal

Plena, plena, plena, va
SanSe en Machuchal

MOURNING IN "LA CASA DE LA PLENA"

(For Héctor René «Tito» Matos Otero,
June 15, 1968 – January 18, 2022)

Me pueden quitar mi casa
me pueden quitar mi tienda
dejarme sin una prenda
sin mi carro, sin mi plaza
pero hay algo que mi raza
protege con gran tesón
del tirano y del ladrón
y es mi plena borinqueña
de la cual nadie se adueña
pues vive en el corazón

—Javier Curet
(From "No Me Quiten Mi Plena")

Plenero, no te quitamos nada—
al contrario, corazones infinitos
te cantamos alabanzas, al ritmo del tambor

you, el ritmo del pueblo
you, who lives in our hearts

Los panderos son mariposas—
thrum of the drums filling La Goyco
sound of a thousand monarch wings

you, el rey de los cueros
you, monarch in flight

Los panderos son estrellas—
your body beneath a galaxy's swirl
buoyed by a sea, dappled mirror of stars

you, una estrella brillante
you, light of a shooting star

Los panderos son una hostia—
every plenero un cura
singing plenas de luto

for you, cantamos tributo
for you, we sing a praise song

TITERES IN DA HOUSE

(For Ponce, Profe, DBird, Isa & Red)

My house is filled with poets,
      New York in their rearview mirror
          as they search
             for homes
                of their juventud,
          and a sacred secret
             that sleeps in la selva.

They roll up in sandals and fedoras
      on a pit stop to forever,
    unfurl tattoos that read like roadmaps,
        drum black nails
          on a table quietly
             turned tambor.

They speak
     names of towns that etch life lines
       on their palms—

          Juncos
          Fajardo
          Guayanilla
          Santurce

        invoked like oraciones

            with a
           Nuyorican
             spin.

We cruise on foot, pass
       graffiti-covered buildings,
       the patios and gardens of La Goyco,
       Casa Laurel en la calle Loíza,
       lamp posts that lean
            and point toward the sea.

Everything seeds verse—
       turtles' sandy nests,
       "the last sandwich in SuperMax",
       mi sancocho…

Coquis sing as evening lands—
       We overfill a van with our voices,
           head for San Juan, wander
           cobblestone streets, stumble
               on metaphors
               in La Plaza de Armas
           where una dama hawks billetes
               de la lotería
          y un señor sells limbers
               de parcha y cherry.

Poets' Passage turns magnet on Tuesday nights
       pulling bards into its bohemian womb—
           red velvet walls
               and filigreed light
                  bathe us
                  in a muse's brew.

       Lady Lee midwifes poems
           from neighborhood
               and nomadic mouths—

A cicada flutters from a shy girl's lips.
A man with a lion's mane roars.
Sabrina flirts
      into the mic
          and we all fall in love

     with words,
        with la gente
          with la vida   en si.

We take turns spitting poems in the spotlight,
    lay our books on Lady Lee's shelves.

The night is electric—alchemy
    of rhythms as primal as heartbeats
    and star glow glistening
    on our skin.

We ramble late-night streets,
    our reflections dancing
      on plate glass windows,
        memories rising
          on aroma of ocean

      as shopkeeps sweep sidewalks
        and clock hands point us home.

WHEN THE MUSE IS A TREE
WITH A DOZEN ARMS REACHING

(For Carlos Sánchez)

A musician paints
    the path of his song
    with the pause between words
        from a wordless poem.

A poet casts words
    into the air,
lets syllables plink
    onto pavement, bounce
    against wind chimes
        in syncopated
            harmony.

Close your eyes.
    Hear the blue sky
        in the long lines
            of the cello.
Follow the wind,
    kites rising
        on crescendo
            of a flute.

A painter hears verse
    voiced in tones
        of tobacco and anise,
    brushes paper
        with mahogany
            and ruby swirls.

A chanteuse eyes a canvas—
        azure sky
                and birthing moon,
scats melodies
        while jazz hands dance
                on the ivories.

OCEAN BREACH:
A TALE OF TWO HOUSES

To the left, a crumble of history:
Moorish arches, mosaic tile,
soaring ceilings, louvered wood
windows, an overhung roof.

Rooms cooled by thick brick and Atlantic breeze,
once filled with patois of país,
sancocho and casabe served on caoba tables
topped with handmade lace.

The house's age is etched on its face
in a multitude of salt-air pocks,
title traversing
generations.

To the right, transplanted northern style—
expanse of thick plate-glass, marble & steel,
hermetically sealed against sound and sea,
a beach-front fortress a half-block wide.

Nighttime dreams are lodged between
parentheses of security cameras and fences
fashioned to stop excess from flowing
towards need.

The sea is the color of dollars
and a million is minimum for a front row seat.
A chorus of *get-out-of-the-way-to-make-room-for-me*
fills the gated streets.

Moonlight floods the old house's roof.
Palm fronds pave the path to the beach.
Investors eye the edge of the sea where fishermen once hauled
crabs that spread across the sand like a giant sea-god's wings.

This collapsing scaffold of the past
stands as testament for those who know
how to see through
twisted histories.

In others' minds, it is an eye-sore
to be razed, a barrier reef
stopping the flow of cash crashing
like a 50-foot wave onto the beach.

An enchantress named *tax-haven* woos
neo-colonizers to this pastiche of paradise
where they feign royalty
from abodes on Kings Court.

Fleeing the rat race, they race like rats to the top of the heap,
displace those who sleep in homes passed down by abuelos,
push them out—to Caguas or Canóvanas,
then curate sea views for a fee.

How do we heal the breach when a floodtide of wealth
greases local wheels with a whiff of the kill?
How do we halt this gluttony for luxury, ocean, and bone,
stop vultures gutting palomas perched in uva de playa trees?

NO SE VENDE (NOT FOR SALE)

Hecha de viento y de playa,
Soy la ola que va a romper.

—iLe (From "*Contra Todo*")

The lady claimed
        she'd bought the beach,
        not just the view
        from her gold & marble condo.

The lady tried
        to silence the glee
        of Boricuas
        playing ball near the dunes.

The lady attacked
        with paper warplanes
        constructed
        from complaint forms.

           ***

We swarmed the beach,
        blanketed the sand with our
        bodies, babies, banderas and beer,
        volleyballs flying
        like defense missiles.

We let the lady know
      the words
      Public & Beach
      are salt & pepper
      in Boricuas' hands.

We let the lady see
      las playas
      belong to
      the people.

      Punto.

HEAT

Sahara sands swirl
across the Atlantic, land
in San Juan, flood
my nostrils, explode
as a sneeze
through my second-floor window,
boomerang back as a shout of *¡Salud!*
by an unseen someone
in Marisol's next-door kitchen.

Our houses fit together
jigsaw puzzle style
along our narrow street,
dead cars and dead birds
sharing the pavement, crushed
beer cans shaping
the weekend's narration.

Friday night, two Peruvian tourists got shot
in front of a club on calle Loíza.
Just hours before, two men from Bayamón
were killed near their car in Hato Rey.

We shake our heads, mutter *¡Ay, bendito!*
as the bells of Parroquia Santa Teresita ring
on Sunday morning.

I wear ear seeds on my auricles,
cultivate inner peace—
We all search for transcendence
and release from constant *traumatic stress*
that refuses to add "*post*" as a prefix.

Disorders form from debris of invasions
and the heat that pools beneath polyester.

The dog days have arrived
early this year,
the mercury hitting 100,
crisis ambiental understood
in nearly any language.

The sun is merciless
on my flat cement roof.

A breeze arrives like a blessing
and Elena's tall caimito tree dances.

The ocean glistens with energy.
I ride the waves, jump with abandon
like the waterlogged pups playing
in the seafoam, chasing balls
their humans throw deep
into the blue-green sea,
tails wagging,
pink tongues panting,
their faith & elation
contagious.

CLIMACTERIC ENCRUSTED IN
A HEAT WAVE

I left because I could
      and the heat was crushing
            my chest, rising from my skin
                  like flame, my body craving chill.

A cold shower trickled delicious,
      a scant breeze lifted sizzle—but
            heat's exhaustion returned swiftly.

I left because I could
      and I'd nearly collapsed
            limping along la calle Loíza.

La Farmacia held my remedy—

Not the plethora of pills and plasters.
      Nor the oils of *culebra o menta, o de tiburón.*
      Not even the fresh citrus
            scent of *agua de azahar*—

But the swoosh of sweet AC.

Yet, I could find relief only so long
      resting on the curve of a cool plastic chair,
           feigning a pharmacy wait.

Back on the street, a steam furnace
      roared through my pores,
           flashes flushed my face.

Inside my house, my body
        like *pan sobao*
                baking in the heat.

I left because I could
        and I needed reprieve
                from fractured ozone
                        and hormones' inferno.

An airplane ticket I'd squirreled away
        became a fan in my sweaty hands,
                crisp parchment splashed with blue—

Cool Pacific mornings, seductive
        sea fog, and a question:
                Y ahora chica, ¿Qué?

Es durante las noches
donde el fantasma de mi nostalgia se siente más.
Noches de bullicio metropolitano
que me hacen añorar
las noches de lluvia y neblina
con el canto de grillos y coquies...

****

It is during the nights
when I feel the ghost of my nostalgia the most.
Nights of urban bustle
that makes me yearn for
the nights of rain and mist
filled with the song of crickets and coquis...

—*Etienne Hernández Velázquez*
(From "El Coqui," translated to
English by *Susana Praver-Pérez*)

THRESHOLDS

In the haze of half dream
        I don't know   where
I am   Oakland or San Juan.

I see   Barbara Lee & Carmen Yulín,
             a pair
          of timbales
      bridging their hands.

I live   on this street   and   across a span
                 of
        trans/continent/al flights
         & satellite beeps.

Some days, I croon
        buenas tardes to a distant ear,
        the sun still
            donning its shoes.

On others, coffee assures me
        Oakland is awake—
           though it still slumbers
               and I am the moon cantando.

In the haze of half sleep
        this poem
appears   like I   appear
      —unannounced—
      gliding along an ocean's rhyme.

Acaríciame con tus palmas—I am
     tired   of half-lived stories.
Sueño despierta—
     tired   of adjectives,   long for
                nouns & verbs.

In the haze of half-light
I wonder   what nouns
             will meet my eyes today,
     what verbs
          will animate

     this grateful body?

MIA TO SJU

Buckled up, we roar
down a runway,
defy gravity with a *whoosh*.
All that follows calls for faith.

The ocean swirls a cavalcade
of teals and blues. Clouds' lavender
shadows stamp the sea...

Shadows—play of light,
real, but lacking body—
like a beloved who lives
in memory
but leaves
aching arms bereft.

A cast of clouds take their turn
on the proscenium:

> Cotton cumulus shapeshift—
> chupacabra, flamboyán, baby
> in its mama's arms.

> Alto cirrus shred like coco
> in a gleaming bowl of blue.

> Cirrostratus fills the sky
> and suddenly, *el cielo*
> *está encancaranublado*...
> tongue-twister dancing
> on my lips.

Islands, some thin as crescent moons,
dot the sea, some with a house
here and there, and I wonder
at such solitude.

Finally, we approach Puerto Rico's shore,
as familiar as my suegra's kitchen.

Condos glimmer like mirages on the sand,
mountains rise as horizon.

Hato Rey's corporate glass and steel
clash with still too many blue tarped roofs.

Highways crisscross and cloverleaf
the island—miraculously afloat.

We glide low above Baldorioty—Route 26,
the beige and orange walk-ups
of Luis Lloréns Torres housing project
endless, like field mushrooms in spring.

Gone is El Fanguito, the sprawling
muddy slum where Lloréns residents'
abuelos once lived,
sewage swirling in brown water
below their stilted shacks.

A sagging horse is tied
to a lamppost in the projects.
I've heard, people bring horses up
into tight apartments, yearning
for a life of the land.

Luis Muñoz Marín International
is within sight—waves crash white,
palms reach to sky,
guide us in with grace.

Wheels meet asphalt
and applause crescendos

like a Hallelujah.

When I was a boy, and you were God, we flew to Puerto Rico. You said:
My grandfather was the mayor of Utuado. His name was Buenaventura.
That means good fortune. I believed in your grandfather's name.
I heard the tree frogs chanting to each other all night. I saw banana
leaf and elephant palm sprouting from the mountain's belly. I gnawed
the mango's pit, and the sweet yellow hair stuck between my teeth.
I said to you: *You came from another planet. How did you do it?*
You said: *Every morning, just before I woke up, I saw the mountains.*

—*Martín Espada* (From "Letter to My Father")

MY NAME CAN DANCE

My name is lush mountains,
        fertile soil, cycles of the moon.
My name can feed a nation
        with plantain and breadfruit.

You can drink water from my name.

Say my name softly
        like a prayer searching for a home
        and I'll shelter you.
Defame my name and my tongue
        will become a machete.

Trampled diphthongs and deleted accents
        are battleships
        breaching my shores.
My name once meant *noble* but was changed
        to *port of riches*
        by those who pillaged my gold.

My name is round syllables,
        sweet orange and light of moon.
My name can dance barefoot
        like Yemayá collecting cowrie shells
        and seafoam.

You can heal wounds with my name.

Say my name softly
        like a lover and light
        will sparkle on calm seas.
Seek to conquer my name
        and blood will churn
        choppy waters.

VISTAS DEL CACIQUE

ca·cique /kə'sēk/
1. (in Latin America or the Spanish-speaking Caribbean)
   a native chief.
2. (in Spain or Latin America)
   a local political boss.
Origin: Spanish or French, **from Taino**. (mid-16th
century)

On hills topped with towns   named
for caciques—Yauco, Jayuya, Guayama, and more—
          network of villages   connecting
first peoples, eyes to the water
                    from thatched roof bohíos,
          oceans of fishes 'neath
                    mountains and clouds.

Atabey, Yucahú,
          sacred cemíes—
deities of earth and heavens
          once reigned.

Broad seas were solo
til white-sailed horizons— men pale
as moonlight
alighting   from ships.

Gods they appeared,
skin like fantasmas.
Awe was their shield
as they raped and enslaved.

Agüeybaná   doubted Spaniards
                as godly,
        tested with water—
                drowned Diego Salcedo,
                        watched his limp body
                        for a trio of days.

        When no life returned,
                        it proved he was mortal,
                and the weight of restraint lifted
                like vapor—

Tainos descended upon the invaders—
        macanas and arrows
                defending Borikén—
        But swords and smallpox outpowered
                the nation.

                ******

On hills topped with towns   named
for los santos—San Juan, San Lorenzo, San Germán, y más—
pueblos con plazas, alcaldías, e iglesias,
fields of cane—cañaverales—
        where stolen Yorubas slaved
                in the heat.

With siglos of melding—often through violence—
        a distinct antillano selfhood arose.

One day in September, el Grito de Lares,
        a yearning for re-birth,
                an end to enslavement,
                        a free Puerto Rico,
                                criollo self-rule.

But sovereignty's questions
        were answered with bullets,
            chorus the clang
                of a prison cell door.

Three decades later, a brief glimpse of freedom,
      but   United States's warships   hijacked
           the island,
      and the reign of a new foreign ruler
           ensued.

******

On white sanded shores, tall waves
      of incursions—
Wyndham, Hyatt, Hilton and more—
"Vistas del Cacique," new luxury housing,
      the very same vistas
           where Tainos once thrived.

¡Qué no tomen ventaja!
      heard en la calle,
          protesting deals
             with sly politicians—
                the newest "caciques,"
                   corruption at core.

A wink or a dollar may loosen las leyes:
      private-own pools   on
                      prime public beaches
      vacation retreats   on
                      vulnerable mangroves.

Where will it end,
        this *Hawai'i'zation*?

When will the carousel
        come to a halt?

Who will lead
        like Agüeybaná?

When will the rightful
        rebellion take hold?

ICONIC

Red and blue
       have faded from the flag—

In their place, three black stripes
       resisting.

      ***

The hands-in-prayer emoji
       has faded on my keyboard—

In its place, icon of a thousand feet
       marching.

A BOUNDLESS RIVER

(After and in homage to Julia de Burgos)

I was born by the mouth
of el Río Grande de Loíza,
where sweet waters kiss Atlantic waves.
I was a rhyme in the river and the river a song
      in my dreams.

Born in the fist of los yanquis,
my island seized sixteen years before,
Spanish coins gathered dust
in a jar by the stove, while my mother boiled
      gandules.

The first of thirteen children,
six died for lack of bread.
Calloused palms held blade and plow
while my hands craved
      paper and pen.

Shapeshifting ribbon,
I became a woman at the waters' edge.
Sharing myself with the glistening flow,
the river woke my heart and caressed
      my limbs.

Fluttering in my chest—a star perched
in a clear blue sky, a pair of moonbeams
and three red rays of dawn—
but despots sought to crush
      my pride.

Big is the Empire we battle,
but bigger is our right to be free!
Don Pedro Albizu Campos's flame
lit a fervent light
      in me

Amidst indignity of foreign rule,
I dreamt birds flying
with both wings. Hija de la Libertad,
I blazed a path to lift up
      women's voice.

On a journey, flowing
among islands north and south,
I loved—body, mind, and soul
pressed to another like the river
      embraces the sea.

But all that I loved turned to anguish—
husbands with names that haunt
my nights, my island
and river in
      conquerors' hands.

Umber and fuchsia words flowing
like the river, my poems
filled pages like oceans fill a bay.
I leave behind these fragments,
      fragrant slivers of me.

I rest by the banks of
el Río Grande de Loíza,
a boundless river,
a raging tributary of tears
      for the pain
        my people endure.

el trajín de tu carne   abandonada
busca su remitente y yo no sé
        a dónde enviarla
a qué calle, morenita
a qué cuadra de qué barrio de cristal
donde esperen el aviso de tu muerte.

****

abandoned   your body billows
in search of its home address
and I don't know
            where to send it
to what street, morenita
to what block of which neighborhood of glass
where they wait for the news of your death.

—*Mayra Santos-Febres*
(From "negra flor de agua   morenita"
translated to English by *Vanessa Pérez-Rosario*)

OBITUARY

Juan
Miguel
Milagros
Olga
Manuel
All died yesterday today
and will die again tomorrow…
All died
waiting for the garden of eden
to open up again
under a new management

—Pedro Pietri (From "Puerto Rican Obituary")

Sovereignty died
on July 25, 1898,
after having died some 400 years before.
Thank God for Resurrection.

Sovereignty unfurled
a red-striped flag
like a phoenix spreads its wings, waved
a *Carta Autonómica* in the heady air.
But the revival didn't last a year.

Sovereignty was gutted
by navy blue and muddy boots
as swiftly as a beheading,
as eerily as an epidemic.
Pesos were replaced with dollars,
a single star
with forty-five.

Sovereignty struggled to stand
and shine but died again and again.

Sovereignty died
on March 21, 1937. Bullets
massacred its Sunday Best,
white lace and guayaberas
red with blood in Ponce.

Sovereignty withered
in a dank prison cell in 1945
for the crime of flying
its flag.

Sovereignty celebrated
its rebirth on July 25, 1952,
rejoiced
at heading its own table.
But while the menu
showcased local tastes,
the chef was shipped in
from the States.

Sovereignty limps
blue lipped and swollen cheeked
down a dusty road
headed to its own memorial.
Some speed by, gape
through rear-view mirrors.
But others pull over,
offer quenepas
from their farms,
sávila to heal lacerations,
and a ride back to San Juan.

STORM WATCH: MONTESSORI STYLE

Luna and Sol sit
    on opposite sides
        of the kitchen table

like their celestial eponyms perch
    on opposite sides
        of the firmament.

Their mother gives them black-lined maps
    of Puerto Rico and a rainbow
        of crayons to fill the empty space

like the coming storm
    will fill the skies
        with torrents and wind.

Dibújala de verde, Mami croons,
    color our island green. And all around it,
        blue—el cielo azul, y el mar también.

Y los ríos—stay within the lines
    when you draw
        the rivers blue—

imbuing her daughters with power
    to hold rivers
        within their banks.

Mami knows the risks
      of rising waters, remembers Hugo, Georges,
           still wears María's scars.

Sol is too young to remember hurricanes—she hums
      as she scrawls gray spirals on cerulean sky, as storm
           clouds thicken outside tight doors.

Luna is old enough to recall María and all the words
      that floated to the murky surface those flooded days—
           mop… thirst… hunger... heat…

The rain begins, beats like a thousand feet running
      across the roof. The wind whines like a siren.
           The lights flicker and die.

Sol lights the battery-powered lantern Papi bought her.
      The yellow glow casts circles on the ceiling,
           as if the ancestors had carved their legends there.

Tell me a story Mami, Sol pleads through the howl of wind,
      cuddled next to her mother, the soft cotton cushions
           of a rattan sofa smooth on her skin.

Mami finds lessons everywhere—
      even in the whirling air.
           Pues… había una vez…

      … a great goddess—Atabey created the heavens.
        With nothing in the barren dark,
           she birthed two magical gods, Yucahú & Guacar.

From his dwelling in the sky, Yucahú awoke the Earth
from its slumber, brought forth cassava,
the sun, the moon, the celestial bodies.

Yucahú opened a cleft in the heavens
from which the first human being came—
He named him Locuo and gave him a soul.

Locuo, filled with joy, roamed the Earth singing
praise to Yucahú, god of the fields,
harmony, and peace.

Yucahú looks out at the world from his throne
atop El Yunque—"The White Lands" named for
the rainforest's circling sea of clouds.

He keeps watch for Guabanseh, goddess of the Wind,
deflects her stormy rage,
protects his beloveds.

So, sleep my sweet daughter—Yucahú sits on his mountain,
you're curled in Mami's arms, and your beautiful
blue rivers are drawn perfectly.

HURRICANE SEASON

Hay un tucu tucu,
    que no tiene nombre,
        a disquiet in my chest—
  a swirl of storms recessed
      in my mind, ticking
        off the list
          of names.
It's September 15th—
we've arrived at "F"—Fiona
    whirling east of the Leewards,
        her eye set on the Greater Antilles.

Five years minus five days ago today,
    "M" morphed into María—
          Mashed
      Mangled
  Mortified.
Forecasters
cup concentric circles
  in digital hands,
    high-res glyphs, not unlike
        glyphs Taínos carved
          in stone— a sideway "S"
    of outstretched arms,
  a woman's face at center—

Guabanseh, fierce goddess of Wind,
    flanked by her twin assistants:
Guataubá and Coatrisque,
    gods of Thunder and Flood.

It is said: when Guabanseh becomes angry,
        she makes the winds and waters move,
                casts houses to the ground, uproots trees.

Hay un tucu tucu
        que no tiene nombre,
                a disquiet in my chest—

Cupboards are filled
        with canned goods.
Candles and kerosene
        stored in sheds.
And an ancient prayer for mercy,
        on three million reverent lips.

WATERCOLORS AFTER THE STORM

Olga paints the aftermath—blue floods
the paper, the sun peeks through an avocado rain.

Her signature fills a corner with pink
like Fiona scrawled gray across the sky.

People with mouths as round as the "O" in "Olga"
stare at streets turned rust-colored rivers.

They slog through rain's wake, straddle downed trees,
return to black houses—the light gone for days.

Patches of yellow shine from Casa Pueblo, walls
painted dusty red rose, its solar plates powering Adjuntas.

Olga paints adjacent towns white-speckled slate—
lightning bugs and lanterns piercing the night.

People cook red beans and rice
in communal kitchens, serve platefuls to neighbors.

Olga highlights flushed faces with fuchsia
as the island swoons in 100-plus heat.

People in Olga's picture wear turquoise and red,
sweep debris out of houses, squeeze water out of beds.

Bridges and roads are smashed—remnants strangle
rivers, mingle with shredded green crops.

People in Olga's painting clear roads
of brown branches and bramble

They boat-rescue families off black-topped roofs,
wishing it were just a déjà vu.

Olga wonders what color to paint exhaustion
that depletes like iguanas raiding a mango tree.

APAGÓN (BLACKOUT)

The glow of my laptop dissolves
in a vortex swirl of black and gray.

Candle in hand, I wander the night
like Diogenes searching for an honest man.

The moon's pale light filigrees
through thick leaves of an almond tree.

Stars, lanterns and lightning bugs sparkle
like diamonds draped on ebony skin.

A string of solar lights flies towards sunrise
like a murmuration of nymphs.

Sean sparks his generator across the street,
small bright island in a sea of ink.

Swaying in a hammock on my porch, I blanket myself
in the comfort of all these chrysalides of light.

MOON SHELL

Juntos en la orilla del mar
dos cangrejos y yo
estuvimos tomando del sol,
mientras la sal
y las espumas
nos bautizaron

—Rebeca Lois Lucret
(From "Bendiciones")

I watch the sea   thinking
    of tides
        that placed me
            like a moon shell
                on the sand

I watch gliders in the air   wind
    in their sails   wondering
        how much   we steer
   &   how much   we're borne
           by the wind

    The sea is a silver mirror—

I watch   my reflection
    the nebulous   sky
        the flutter
    of palm trees
    feel the pull   this island

        I watch

REASONS FOR RETURNING

(After Ocean Vuong)

A rooster crows in the dark.
The first pink rays filter through palm fronds.
Un café, a cool cotton bata, mi terraza. El barrio begins to stir.
I celebrate waking while the cock thinks nothing of his *cú-cu-rú-cu-cú.*

I write in the peace of dawn while the world flames in war.
Words sometimes pour out of me in perfect rhyme—& it's awesome.
When you love an island, its sounds become your voice.

San Juan's air carries oceans.
We carry on—mercy & compassion are what saves us.
I make amends for the messes I've made.
This life is the only one I have.

The scent of sofrito on calle Loíza makes me hungry.
My favorite telenovela is el bochinche del barrio.
The coquis' song is my favorite lullaby.

A storm rains warm on my shoulders.
Winter & Summer are twins.
Bomba & Plena scaffold the island's rhythms.
Mi amor, multiplied a million times, equals family.

Graffiti on broken buildings becomes *Art* when you squint just right.
Se Vende signs, scrawled in red paint, drip like wounds needing healing.
The electric grid is a nightmare, but we've learned how to dance in the dark.

I hold this fractured island in my heart, unbroken.
I made a promise.

THE BACKSTORY

In 1978, I fell in love with José de Jesús Pérez, a proud Boricua from Agua-dilla. And as I did, I fell in love with Puerto Rico. Actually, there would have been no way to marry José without also "marrying" Puerto Rico. Although we were living in California, the island was deeply present in our lives, and we were frequently present on the island visiting José's large, close-knit family. Puerto Rico soon became heart and home for me as well.

Not long into our relationship, José's desire to return to the island he had left a decade earlier became contagious. In the late 1980s, we started to make plans to move to Puerto Rico. For many years we were on the verge of owning a home of our own there, but for various reasons, our dream didn't come to fruition at that time.

Housing wasn't our main barrier to return, however. The reality of trying to make a living in a nation falling further and deeper into financial strati-fication and hardship due to exploitation inherent in its colonial relation-ship with the United States, was daunting. And still is. As I write this in 2023, the median household income in Puerto Rico is approximately $22,000 per year and the cost of living is high.

Economic considerations have been one of the main reasons that, starting in the mid-1900s, Puerto Ricans began emigrating from the island in sig-nificant numbers. In the 1950s, the flow of Puerto Ricans to the United States was so dramatic that it became known as the "Great Migration." An estimated 470,000 people—or 21 percent of the island's total popula-tion—left Puerto Rico for the U.S. between 1950 and 1960. Another 10 percent of the population left during the following 10 years.

There was another sharp uptick in departures after September 2017's Hurricane María left the archipelago without light and water. In some areas, particularly mountainous towns like Utuado, residents went an entire year without electricity. Many people never received funds due to them from FEMA and were unable to rebuild their homes. Others, without employment in the aftermath of the hurricane, lost their homes to foreclosure which had been on the rise since the global financial downturn in 2008, but was now epidemic.

And as these conditions forced many Puerto Ricans to leave the island, vulture capitalists (deep-pocketed investors who profit off natural and financial disasters) started pouring in, buying up the best land, gentrifying traditional neighborhoods, driving up rents, and thereby pushing even more local folks out.

But despite all of this, and even with a net migration rate that has tended towards the U.S.—so much so that as we turned the corner into the 21st century, the number of Puerto Ricans in the States surpassed the number of Puerto Ricans on the island—there has always been a significant number of people—both island and diaspora born—who have *returned against the flow* for a variety of reasons—including the desire to contribute their presence and energies to the nation.

José never got a chance to fulfill his dream of moving back to Puerto Rico; he died in San Francisco in 2007 after battling a long illness. As I scattered his ashes in the places he loved on the island, I made a promise to one day return and replant roots as he always wanted.

In the ensuing years, I was too busy working and raising our then adolescent son on my own to do anything towards fulfilling that promise other than visit my in-law family regularly. But about a decade ago, I brushed off our shared dream, let it rattle around in my head, checked out houses and apartments whenever visiting the island, browsed the *Clasificados* . . .

Then one day in 2021, an apartment was listed for sale in a San Juan neighborhood where many members of my in-law family have lived for decades. For numerous reasons, it felt like a now-or-never moment. So, with a niece and nephew on the island serving as my "boots on the ground," I bought the apartment (half of a two-family house actually), sight unseen.

I've spent considerable time in Puerto Rico over the past 45 years, but having my own home has sharpened my perceptions of the island's day-to-day realities. I love my domestic routine, but with it comes a multitude of challenges. It is now on me to fix the electricity (which blew on my third night in the house), the plumbing (that offered up just a trickle of cold water), and deal with a myriad of other issues related to living in an old building on a colonized island that feels supply-chain deficits all the more acutely because the cabotage aspects of the U.S. Jones Act makes everything on the island more expensive and harder to acquire.

I am certainly far from alone in this frustrating struggle—millions of Puerto Ricans navigate a fractured infrastructure, austerity measures occasioned by default on a $72 million debt and resultant fiscal control board policies, contend with blackouts, water shortages, craters in the streets and sidewalks, etc. And they have been doing so daily for a very long time. I am lucky to have family, friends, and neighbors to help and guide me. I learn from them, take their lead.

As poets tend to do, I found myself writing about my experiences and observations. And thus, this book was born. I hope my work will add something of use to the conversation about the crucial situation in which Puerto Rico finds itself in this moment of history, pivoting on the point of a pin.

ACKNOWLEDGMENTS

Many thanks to J.K. Fowler and Nomadic Press for first accepting *Return Against the Flow* for publication, and to Diane Goettel and Black Lawrence Press for welcoming my collection when Nomadic ceased publishing in February 2023. What a powerful experience of community when two presses work together to have your back!

Much appreciation to the composers, poets, and prose writers whose words I have placed as epigraphs among my own poems to create bridges and intertextual conversations. (Details regarding their pieces and publishing credits to follow.)

Much gratitude to friends, family, and the various writing communities that encourage my work and with whom I have fine-tuned many of these poems from various vantage points.

Many thanks to Tanya Torres for painting the cover art specially for my book. It is a visual delight and captures the mood in which so many of these poems were written.

Everlasting appreciation to my family, friends, and neighbors who appear in many of these poems. Thank you for allowing me to shine literary light on you.

And of course, to my late husband José de Jesús Pérez, whose love for the island of his birth became contagious, and to Puerto Rico for embracing me as a daughter nearly half a century ago—*mucho, mucho amor!*

Thank you to the following journals and anthologies for first publishing the following poems from this book (either in current or previous iterations):

About Place Journal—"No Small Love," "Navegando," "Still(with)Life–Woman with Rooster"

great weather for MEDIA's anthology: *A Shape Produced by a Curve*—"Títeres in da House"

La Raíz Magazine—"A Boundless River"

Nomadic Press—1) From my first full-length collection of poetry *Hurricanes, Love Affairs and Other Disasters*: "Return Against the Flow," "Better Homes & Gardens: Puerto Rico Edition, "Castles in the Air," "Caminante," "Sancocho," "Ode to Titi" 2) From the anthology, *The Town*: "Thresholds"

Pease Press / Write Now! SF Bay's anthology: *Essential Truths*)—"A Mi Querido Negrito en Su Día"

Peggy Robles-Alvarado "No Small Voices on this Bridge" Project—"Through the Cracks"

The Acentos Review—"Carta de Amor," "Beauty," "A Storm Named Maria," "Reasons for Returning," "Dancing Bomba in La Goyco," "Mourning in 'La Casa de la Plena,'" "Ocean Breach: A Tale of Two Houses"

CREDITS

(In alphabetical order by first name)

Anna Andresian

Autobiographical vignette written for this project. Used with permission of the author.

Denice Frohman

Excerpt from "Puertopia". Originally published online in *Kweli Journal* and in print in the anthology *What Saves Us: Poems of Empathy and Outrage in the Age of Trump* (Northwestern University Press). Used with permission of the author.

Etienne Hernández

Excerpt from "El Coquí." Used with permission of its author.

Translation to English by Susana Praver-Pérez.

iLe (Ileana Cabra Joglar)

Excerpt from "Caníbal" from the album *iLevitable*. Used with permission of the composer.

Excerpt from "Contra Todo" from the album *Almadura*. Used with permission of the composer.

Isa Anastasia Rivas

Excerpt from "the poet leads me through Santurce (dedicated to Susana Praver-Pérez)." Used with permission of the author.

Excerpt from "Yo Veo." Used with permission of the author.

Javier Curet

Excerpt from "No Me Quite Mi Plena." Used with permission of the composer.

Susana Praver-Pérez is a bilingual poet and visual artist. A former Physician Assistant and Associate Medical Director at *La Clínica de la Raza* in Oakland, California, Susana left medicine in 2021 after four decades of community service, to pursue her passion for poetry on a full-time basis. Her first full-length collection, *Hurricanes, Love Affairs, and Other Disasters* earned the PEN Oakland Josephine Miles Award for Excellence in Literature (2022).

To date, Susana's other honors include the San Fransico/Nomadic Press Literary Award (2021), a residency at the Bethany Arts Center, and nominations for various prizes, including a Pushcart. But the rewards she values most are those that come from learning she has moved someone deeply with her poems.

* 9 7 8 1 6 2 5 5 7 0 8 3 3 *